020 7839 7551
gallery@chrisbeetles.com
www.chrisbeetles.com

'New Donald McGill' images © Pharos International Ltd. 2006

ISBN · 1 871136 96 2

Introduction by John Russell Taylor
Life Events by John Henty
Extracts from *The Art of Donald McGill* by George Orwell, *Horizon*, 1941

Design by Edwina Freeman
Photography by Giles Huxley-Parlour
Printing by BAS Printers

Compiled and Edited by Edwina Freeman

THE MICHAEL WINNER COLLECTION OF

DONALD McGILL

Foreword
by Michael Winner

Henpecked husbands. Honeymooners. Married couples at war. Mothers-in-law. Very fat women. Donald McGill, king of the seaside postcard, made fun of them all. And he always threw in a saucy joke for good measure.

I like McGill's work because I'm extremely juvenile (it's one of my few qualities). It typifies an age when political correctness, thank goodness, did not exist. There's nothing more tedious than political correctness. It's the triumph of the smug over the normal people of the world. Why shouldn't we laugh at fat people? Newspapers are always printing pictures with rude captions about me being fat. I don't care! If I was a woman they wouldn't dare! That's the reason I went around grinning endlessly – and sometimes laughing out loud – as I sought out original McGill postcard watercolours. I bought them. I hoarded them. The result is that I own 200 McGill originals – the world's largest collection. They show a history of Great Britain from around 1900 to 1962.

They're quite superb.

As well as McGill's classic double entendres accompanying pictures of fat ladies on the beach, there are also delightful pictures of children, sentimental ones of soldiers and wives during the two world wars, and Hitler hanging out his smalls on the Siegfried Line. They are strongly and brightly coloured. They have immense life and vivacity. They are the music hall bawdy joke transferred to postcards. They are among my favourite paintings. They come from a long line of naughty art typified by Thomas Rowlandson and James Gillray in the 18th century.

Perhaps it was Donald McGill's popularity that caught the attention of the do-gooders. He produced 12,000 designs and it's estimated that 350 million of his postcards have been sent. Punch magazine said he was the 'most popular, hence most eminent English painter of the century'. Seaside resorts from Blackpool to Bournemouth,

Margate to Cleethorpes had censorship committees full of busybodies watching out for McGill's art and that of his followers.

McGill himself spoke of his formula for success. 'Take a woman with luscious curves, for and aft. That's essential because people don't care for thin females – if they did, how would the manufacturers of falsies get a living? Dress the woman in the brightest of colours. Add a caption capable of a double meaning and you have a comic card that, by all the rules, should sell at least 50,000 copies.'

McGill divided his cards into three categories: mild, medium and strong. Not surprisingly the 'strong' ones sold the best. He was old-fashioned music hall in pictures. He was Frankie Howerd, Benny Hill, Max Miller and Kenneth Williams in pick-up-at-the-newsagent form. He was a visual representation of the plays of Joe Orton and the lyrics of Ian Dury.

McGill captured a forbidden world of British humour in an age of family values and comparative innocence, when sex was seen as naughty. It wasn't everywhere, like it is today.

Donald McGill was a British hero to me. He's always made me laugh. At least I can do something about the burial site. I shall be arranging and paying for a headstone to be erected to this great artist. It's only right that someone who gave so much pleasure is remembered at the spot where he lies. Now what double entendres can I think of to engrave on the marble headstone?

Introduction
by John Russell Taylor

In a sense, it's all down to George Orwell. Not completely, of course: Donald McGill would have existed, and probably been remembered, even without Orwell's famous September 1941 essay in *Horizon*, "The Art of Donald McGill". And indeed, Orwell writes about McGill strictly as *primus inter pares*, though he does distinctly state "I have associated [seaside postcards] especially with the name of Donald McGill because he is not only the most prolific and by far the best of contemporary postcard artists, but also the most representative, the most perfect in the tradition. Who Donald McGill is I do not know..."

Despite this, let's face it, slightly qualified approval, it can safely be said that Orwell discovered McGill, was the first authority to pick him out for special notice, and publicise him as an artist worth the serious note of serious people. The first book about McGill, Arthur Calder-Marshall's *Wish You Were Here* (1966) inevitably begins by quoting a whole crucial paragraph from Orwell, though immediately going on to remark that it is "a typical Orwellian pronouncement, a compound of shrewdness and nonsense". Elfreda Buckland's *The World of Donald McGill* (1984) has as its first epigraph a quotation from Orwell (and as its second one from Calder-Marshall). And just try checking McGill on the Internet, and see how far you get without becoming entangled with Orwell.

All credit to Orwell for picking McGill out of the host of virtually anonymous artists who worked in the despised form of the saucy postcard. But of course such a unique position carries its responsibilities as well as its glories. If we see McGill's work, still, largely through Orwell's eyes, what if he got it wrong? Praised it too little, or too much, or all for the wrong reasons? 2006, after all, is very different from 1941: not only in another century, but another millennium. Our views of obscenity are as different as our views on what is or is not art. Or so we half like, half fear to think.

It is very difficult now to imagine that the simple, implicational ribaldry of McGill could ever have brought him into court on a serious charge (no, not that kind of serious charge, missus), while, in an era when Gilbert and George are accepted as modern classics, it seems curious to say the least that Orwell should have made such heavy weather of labelling it as "art".

Presumably McGill himself would have found all this fuss and bother quite mysterious. Indeed, we know that he was quite nonplussed when, in 1954, not that long before the start of the Swinging Sixties, a group of McGill cards were found guilty at Lincoln Quarter Sessions of obscenity, and McGill and his partner in their production company were fined £50 with costs of £25. Of course, it was not so much the money as the shame of it all, and even though the defendants were persuaded that it was wise tactics to plead guilty, McGill felt aggrieved that something so essentially innocent as a slightly smutty double entendre should call down on its head the full wrath of the law. Still, we do have to remember that shortly before, the ineffable Max Miller had been banned for years from the wireless for telling, on something like *Workers' Playtime*, the one about meeting a pretty girl on a narrow plank across a river and not knowing whether to block her passage or toss himself off.

As *Take It From Here* once had it, he who laughs last has just seen the dirty meaning. And yes, of course, it was part of the seaside postcard just as much as the music hall that the dirty meaning was put there deliberately for those who could see it, but also on the assumption that there were many who couldn't and wouldn't. When Marie Lloyd was called down on her song about the girl who "sits among the cabbages and peas", she satisfied criticism by changing it to "she sits among the cabbages and leeks". Obviously her popular audience got the point of both versions, but there were probably many too naïve, or too refined, to get it from either. And a similar situation clearly existed with seaside postcards: they did not need to be labelled "Adults Only" because childish innocence would not be affronted by something it did not understand in the first place. Just like an off-colour gag in a panto.

All this is of direct relevance to the understanding, if not necessarily the appreciation, of Donald McGill. Born in 1875, he lived in his 87 years through the heyday of Marie Lloyd and the oldtime musical, the invention and perfection of the modern pantomime, with all its sex-reversals and double entendres, the rise and fall of Max Miller and the Crazy Gang, and into the domination of every front room in the country by the television in the corner. And kept pace with nearly all of them, though he probably felt that television was a sad fall from grace. For television, despite its moments of social boldness, was in his day very namby-pamby and careful not to offend. After all, would you want something as rude as sexual innuendo in your living room, and have to watch and react to it in front of the kiddies?

Probably not, given the general level of hypocrisy in 20th-century Britain. Of course, you might not mind it too much if it came through your letterbox, aimed in your direction by some temporarily liberated friend on a seaside holiday. The whole point of the exercise, after all, was to embarrass the recipient, force him (or indeed her, in the days of Elsie and Doris Waters) to rush to the front door and gather up the post before the children could get their hands on it. It was like going, as I did as a child, *en famille* to see an evening's variety at, say, the theatre of Butlin's Holiday Camp, Skegness, finding that Frankie Howerd in person was much ruder than he was on the wireless, and having to pretend, husband and wife in front of each other, and both in front of child, that you did not really understand the ruder jokes, and certainly did not find them funny.

Of course McGill, as prime creator of postcard ruderies, knew perfectly well what he was doing: it was an open secret that he shared with his audience. What was wrong with the whistle-blowers who brought him to court was that they were not playing the game. It is highly unlikely that any adults receiving an image of a red-faced, corpulent middle-aged man with a little boy sheltered beneath his spreading waistline, gazing into the distance and complaining "Can't see my little Willy", were so innocent as not to realize that there was a double meaning there somewhere, but they could always pretend not to see beyond the simple visual joke, and, mercifully, were presented with nothing about which the children were guaranteed to ask awkward questions.

Before we get too superior about this not-in-front-of-the-children attitude, we should recognise that even in our own time there was a rumpus about a Benetton photographic billboard showing a newborn baby with his umbilical cord uncut, and the reason urged for its suppression was not that it was in any way indecent, but that it might lead to children's asking parents embarrassing questions about what that strange appendage was. No one could accuse McGill of having designs on the sexual education of our children. What he was interested in was half-revealing, half-concealing a few adult secrets, and making grown-ups laugh, albeit shamefacedly, at something the kids were not only too young to understand, but too innocent even to recognise the existence of.

And of course, even that was not strictly true. If McGill's cards appealed as much to children as to adults, it was partly at least because children progressively recognised them as a key to adult understanding. Obscene they seldom are by any sensible definition, but they are often smutty in a very childish way - the acme of sophistication for some little person who has just progressed beyond the unspeakable rudeness of wee-wee and poo-poo, and found that there are still ruder things to say which might have something to do with that greater mystery of SEX. Even at his most suggestive, McGill preserves an innocent, childlike (if not downright childish) charm. He is a bit like the children in *Dear Octopus* who get the idea that "district nurse" is an unmentionable term, and are disappointed when they shout it out to find that the only response is "What about the district nurse, darling?"

That said, it must be admitted also that in many respects McGill is very much of his period. These days there is little of a sexual or scatological nature in McGill jokes that even a nun would find shocking. (Indeed, maybe a nun is the last person who would: when Hitchcock decided to test the apparently ladylike Grace Kelly by telling off-colour jokes in her presence, her immediate response was "You must remember, Mr Hitchcock, that as a convent-educated girl I've heard far worse than that!") No, what we might well find shocking is his complete political incorrectness or, worse, complete unawareness that such a thing as political correctness exists. Because, naturally, in his day it didn't.

It is curious that as one aspect of McGill's legacy gets milder and milder, another aspect becomes more and more questionable. It was not a question for Orwell in 1941: in his first paragraph he himself refers unselfconsciously to "nigger minstrels", and though he lists the stereotypes that reign in McGill's world, where young men are always randy ("They're honeymooners." "Yes, it's sticking out a mile.") and middle-aged men are always henpecked and ineffectually libidinous, while young women are innocently provocative and older women are either dried-up spinsters or inflated harridans, rolling-pin (metaphorically at least) always in hand, he does not seem to have any rooted objection to them.

Nor, I think, should we. They are not, after all, unpleasantly meant. They are part of a great tradition that goes back at least to Chaucer, and had been transmitted to McGill via Shakespeare, Goldsmith, Dickens, Gilbert and Sullivan and hundreds of other perfectly respectable literary figures. If we are going to bundle it all away out of sight at this late date, we are surely shutting the stable door after the hobby-horse has fled.

Back in those far-off days when *The Black and White Minstrel Show* was among television's highest-rated attractions, a lady from Brixton wrote to *The Times* saying that every time the show was on she sat in front of her set, tears streaming down her face for the affront that was being offered to her people. The editor - one hardly dares admit it now - did not have much sympathy. We were all of us, he observed, subject to stereotyping. Nobody, not even mothers-in-law, took it very seriously if mothers-in-law were generally characterised as monstrous, as that was all part of life's rich tapestry. And if one belonged to a group which was generally characterised as happy, laughing, and regularly contributing to the gaiety of nations, then surely there were many worse places to be.

I suspect that Donald McGill's attitude was much the same - if he ever queried the basic assumptions of his chosen form at all. But then, why should he? It would have been like questioning the pantomime convention that, while Aladdin was played by a shapely young woman in tights, his mother Widow Twanky was inevitably presented as a grotesquely made up, middle-aged man in drag. Of course mothers-in-law were holy terrors, newly-marrieds were frozen in embarrassment and long-married couples were locked in deadly enmity, mashers (McGill went far enough back to use the term in all seriousness) were always sneaking a peak up busty young women's skirts while everyone else was trying to gauge what, if anything, covered a Scotsman's modesty beneath his kilt. (Scots, of course, always wore kilts, or how would you know they were Scottish?) Clergymen were always blithering idiots, spinsters spiky, unsuccessfully man-hungry, and ready to disapprove of anything.

Apart from the Scots and the occasional Paddy, there were surprisingly few national or ethnic stereotypes: few comical blacks or Indians, or even, a common target in the years between Fagin and Svengali, Jews. This probably had little to do with any special sense of delicacy on McGill's part, but simply that, even back then, such subjects bordered too closely on the political, and therefore were by definition not funny, or not unless you were a satirist   aiming at a sophisticated audience. And   t h a t clearly McGill never was. The only occasions (apart from a brief flirtation, perhaps ironic, with Lloyd George: an empty bed captioned "There's no need to be short of money, Or for joining the 'great unemployed', Just fill this and you get thirty shillings By GEORGE! It is joy una-LLOYD!!") that anything like politics impinges on his work are during the two world wars. And even then, the comment is mild and general: surely Hitler himself could not have been too offended by a graphic illustration of the song about hanging out the washing on the Siegfried Line, which shows him gazing in mystification or alarm at a washing line covered with smalls, each of which has a swastika prominently inscribed on it?

I have a gay English friend, long resident in New York and the maker of some of the most intelligent and cultivated porno films ever, who always says that what he is really nostalgic for is oldtime furtiveness, because everything was much more fun then. McGill must be seen in that light: the proper reaction to his best jokes is a stifled giggle rather than an open guffaw. After all, what would the neighbours think? What would the wife think? Or, even more vital a matter, what would hubby think if he fully realized that you

understood and enjoyed these prime examples of smoking-room, men-only humour? Yes, to an extent full enjoyment of McGill requires a certain flexing of the historical imagination. But then enough Old English hypocrisy is bred in the bone of us all to ensure that this is not too demanding an exercise.

And there is much of entertainment value to be picked up along the way. Fossils of long forgotten slang, for instance. Did you know that "looking a sketch" was a term of mild opprobrium between the wars? I didn't, until McGill told me, by observing that "Many girls look a picture at night, but they look a sketch in the morning". And at once one can imagine someone from a corner of Mapp and Lucia saying "My dear, did you see the way she was made up? She looked an absolute sketch!"

But enough of this sociological tittle-tattle. It is specifically "The Art of Donald McGill" that Orwell claimed to be considering, and that should no doubt primarily interest us. Inevitably, the question which has so often been raised lately in relation to Turner Prize-winners comes up: But is it art? Orwell did not claim much for McGill on purely artistic grounds. He admitted that McGill had a distinctive and instantly recognisable style. He added that "Anyone who examines his post cards in bulk will notice that many of them are not despicable even as drawings, but it would be mere dilettantism to pretend that they have any direct aesthetic value."

It depends what you mean by "aesthetic value". Orwell admits that "McGill is a clever draughtsman with a real caricaturist's touch in the drawing of faces..." But otherwise he seems to have real difficulty with the general lack of beauty in McGill's work. He writes of "the hideousness of the colours", and adds "The designs, like those of a child, are full of heavy lines and open spaces, and all the figures in them, every gesture and attitude, are deliberately ugly, the faces grinning and vacuous, the women monstrously parodied, with bottoms like Hottentots."

The key word there, surely, is "deliberately". It is undeniable that McGill has a particularly merciless eye for every lubricious detail: the precise way the fabric of a dress stretches across the behind of an overweight woman, or moulds around the ripe-melon-breasts of a well-endowed young woman. The point is reinforced, but not exclusively made by the captions. "Oh, Painter," says the bulging housewife to the alarmed house-painter, "I want you to touch up the place where my husband put his hand last night!", "I think they're wonderful!" exclaims the debauched-looking man, fingering the young woman's pearl necklace but gazing intently somewhere lower down. "Many a battle has been fought under this grand old flag!" announces the fat lady with a Union Jack draped over her ample curves.

Ugly? Well, maybe. Vulgar? Decidedly yes. At least I think so, but perhaps it is just my dirty mind. The skill is in the ambiguity. And if the pictures are expressive without the words, yet perfectly fitted to their captions, then that must betoken an artist, and an artistry, of some kind at work. Not one, surely, that would appeal to people from the top drawer. But then, after all, there are many things in this world much worse than not being from the top drawer. And the bargain basement is much more fun.

JOHN RUSSELL TAYLOR IS ART CRITIC OF *THE TIMES*.

Donald McGill 1875 – 1962
Life Events by John Henty

Perhaps George Orwell could be forgiven for writing in 1941 "Who Donald McGill is, I do not know." Thanks to Orwell, Donald McGill himself remained faceless and no attempt was made to actually encounter the person behind the humour until in 1984, educationalist Elfreda Buckland, 'fired' by her husband's long-standing interest in McGill, determined to put the record straight in her colourful book *The World of Donald McGill*. Wisely, she sought out McGill's daughters for an informed and family view of their remarkable father. It was with confidence and knowledge, therefore, that she wrote in her introductory paragraph "To suggest that he was a brand name or a team, was far off the mark. Donald McGill was one man, a very special man, and this book attempts to put his life's work in context."

It succeeded and for that reason alone I have chosen to make detailed reference to it in compiling this chronology. There are gaps but remember, as *The Independent on Sunday* tellingly recorded in October 2005; "In life, Donald McGill was a bookish but twinkle-eyed man who lived all his life in the London suburbs of Blackheath and Streatham and who resembled, in his quiet, dapper way, nothing so much as a small-town solicitor". This is a brief, incomplete record then of that "quiet, dapper way".

1875 : Donald Fraser Gould McGill born on January 25 in the Regent's Park area of North London. He grew up with his three surviving brothers and three unmarried sisters in St. John's Park, Blackheath. Educated at Stratheden House and later …

1890 : Blackheath Proprietary School

1891 : Sustained an injury to his left ankle during a rugby match. Subsequently he had to have his foot amputated. Attended Art School in Bennett Park, Blackheath, but left after a year because "he did not like the syllabus"

1892: First published work in *The Joker* magazine

1893 : Joined a firm of naval architects, Maudsleys in London. He then became articled as an engineering draughtsman to the reconstructed Thames Ironworks, Shipbuilding and Engineering Company until 1907

1900 : In August, married Florence Isabel Hurley, one of three daughters of Alfred Ambrose Hurley, proprietor of the former Crowder's Music Hall in Stockwell Street, Greenwich

1901 : Daughter, Mary Rosina McGill born in May

1904 : Daughter, Margaret Elizabeth Shuter McGill born in November. First postcards published when working part-time as a freelance until 1907 for the Pictorial Postcard Company run by a man of German extraction, Max Honnest

1908 : Joined Percy Hutson and his brother when they took over the Pictorial Postcard Company – Percy having been a representative for Honnest

1910 : First association with Joseph Ascher who was a customer of the Hutsons. Ascher arrived in England from Germany in 1902 and described himself as a 'Fine Art Publisher'. He offered McGill six shillings for the copyright of any card which he accepted. Six cards a week were produced until the outbreak of the First World War when Ascher was interned as an enemy alien

1914 : At the age of 39 joined American Robert McCrumb, who, with his wife, ran the Inter-Art Company, a publishing enterprise with a warehouse in Nassau Road, Barnes, SW13. McGill turned out an average of nine cards a week for the next 17 years

1931 : Moved to Bennett Park, Blackheath. Left Inter-Art. "There was a clean-up and they would not let me draw people with red noses, women in bathing costumes with cleavage. It was so ridiculous – I resigned."

1932 : Robert McCrumb retired and sold Inter-Art

1934 : Joseph Ascher (now Asher) returned to England, a refugee from Nazi Germany and set up the firm of D. Constance Ltd. at 3 to 4 Ivy Lane, London EC4

1936 : D. Constance Ltd. introduced the 'New McGill Series' – sole publishers of all New (emphasised) Donald McGill Comics. McGill entered into a 'gentleman's' agreement with a nominal single shareholding in the company

1939 : 64 years of age, retired to Guildford, Surrey, from Blackheath, where he worked as a temporary clerk with the Ministry of Labour until 1944 when he started drawing again

1941 : George Orwell wrote in the magazine *Horizon*: "McGill is a clever draughtsman with a real caricaturist's touch in the drawing of faces but the special value of his postcards is that they are so completely typical"

1951 : Upon the death of Joseph Asher, took over the management of D. Constance Ltd. at the age of 76 with Ernest Maidment as General Manager

1952 : Wife, Florence, died of cancer after over 50 years of marriage

1954 : On July 15 pleaded Guilty at Lincoln Quarter Sessions to breaking the 1857 Obscene Publications Act with designs for four postcards. Fined £50 plus £25 costs

1955 : Beat the panel in the TV programme *What's My Line* and answered Gilbert Harding's aggressive "So you do those dirty postcards ?" with a dignified "No, I am a seaside artist."

1957 : Postcard work featured in TV programme *This Week* on Associated Rediffusion

1962 : Died on October 13 at St James' Hospital, Balham, of a gastric ulcer and diverticulutis. He was buried in Streatham Park cemetery, leaving 200 unfinished sketches and postcard designs for the following season already completed

SEASIDE

"McGill is a clever draughtsman with a real caricaturist's touch in the drawing of faces, but the special value of his post cards is that they are so completely typical. They represent, as it were, the norm of the comic post card. Without being in the least imitative, they are exactly what comic post cards have been any time these last forty years, and from them the meaning and purpose of the whole genre can be inferred."

George Orwell, 'The Art of Donald McGill'

1

'I feel a lethargy creeping over me.'
'I don't wonder. This darn beach is crawling alive with 'em!'

2

3

4

I thought I was going to click, girls,
But the dirty son-of-a-gun,
He only pinched my cornet
Then skipped towards the setting sun!

I think I shall click if I stick it out
a few days more

I don't know what the vicar would
think of this place, but it's ok by me!

5

The boating is lovely here.
The sea is just as smooth as a baby's bottom le!

6

It's a wise child that knows his own father!

7

I'm getting that schoolgirl complexion all over down here!

8

**Look at me after a week here –
And I came down for my rheumatism too!**

9

**There's no news in the paper so –
I'm looking at the comic strip!**

10

I've fallen in a big way for a girl down here!

12

Me and my donkey

11

I'm coming home by rocket

13

I'm taking daddy for a bathe

14

Me an' my gal are down here

15

I'm feeling a perfect kid again here

16

I don't need a barometer.
I can look into a girls' eyes and tell whether!

17

There's a lovely smooth sea here,
with a nice sandy bottom

18

I've just arrived!

19

No one knew me when I came down here,
but now I'm one of the most prominent men in the place

20

'I've always sworn I'd never kiss a man till I was engaged
'Well that cuts me out, doesn't it?'
'Oh, I am engaged now!'

21

This place is ruining me for office life!

22

I'm getting a good sniff of the briny down here!

24

I've just arrived with a heart full of love
and a pocket full of money

23

I'm sitting in the only bit of
shade on the beach!

26

Nothing more at present

25

Me and my donkey

27

I'm enjoying the see-knee-ry here!

NEWLYWEDS & NAIVETÉ

"Sex.- More than half, perhaps three-quarters, of the jokes are sex jokes, ranging from the harmless to the all but unprintable. First favourite is probably the illegitimate baby...Also newlyweds, old maids, nude statues and women in bathing-dresses. All of these are *ipso facto* funny, mere mention of them being enough to raise a laugh. Conventions of the sex joke:

    i) Marriage only benefits women. Every man is plotting seduction and every woman is plotting marriage.

No woman ever remained unmarried voluntarily."

George Orwell, 'The Art of Donald McGill'

28

'Fancy wanting to kiss me! I didn't think you were that kind!!'

'Oh, I'm much kinder than that – you wait till it gets dark!'

29

I'm glad Mother insisted on my bringing
this book with me!

30

'Very handy folding bed, Sir,
if you're furnishing a small flat.'
'And - er - do instructions go with it?'

31

I and My Bird!

32

Oh Girls! I've been kissed on the
breakwater!!

33

'Is it true that sailors have a wife
in every port?'
'Not with me - I ain't been
in every port!'

34

What my boss says is right.
He certainly makes advances!

35

I'm afraid I've run out of talcum powder madam, but if you'd walk this way – !

36

Good heavens Madam, didn't your mother tell you anything?

37

'Don't George, Mother wouldn't like it!'

'Good heavens, you don't suppose I'd do it to your mother, do you?'

38

39

40

Me? I can show you more things
than the birds and the bees ever dreamt of!!

I met her in the park,
She looked so very sweet,
Then when it was getting dark
I kissed her on the seat

It's most confusing! Mother tells me one
thing and you tell me another!

"ii) Sex-appeal vanishes at about the age of twenty-five.
Well-preserved and good-looking people beyond their first youth are never represented. The amorous honeymooning couple reappear as the grim-visaged wife and shapeless, moustachioed, red-nosed husband, no intermediate stage being allowed for."

George Orwell, 'The Art of Donald McGill'

41

'The bride was given away by her father'
'That's more than your father did – he let me find out for myself!'

42

43

44

'What would you do if I died, John?'
'My dear, I should go crazy!'
'Would you marry again?'
'Oh I shouldn't go as crazy as all that!!'

'Have you read about that machine that can tell if a man's lying or not?'
'Read about it? Great Scott! I married it!!'

It's not what she's got that you haven't.
It's what you've got that <u>she</u> hasn't!!

45

Old or young,
tall or short

Pick 'em out
at random

This bally
town seems
full of men

Whose wives don't understand 'em!

46

Come on! You don't want silk –
you want muzzlin!

48

I never knew anyone who knew less about
more things than you don't!!

47

My wife and I

Are very much
in love,

But not with each other!

MARRIAGE & HOME LIFE

"Home Life. Next to sex, the henpecked husband is the favourite joke. Conventions:
i) There is no such thing as a happy marriage.
ii) No man ever gets the better of a woman in argument."

George Orwell, 'The Art of Donald McGill'

49

**There's only one thing prevents me calling you a bare-faced liar –
you haven't shaved this morning!**

50

Have you missed a patient by
any chance? Because someone's
run off with my wife!

51

Was it dark!! Well I bumped into my
husband in the shed and he raised
his hat and apologised!!

52

'Your husband seems very queer. I hope his
affairs are all in order?'
'What d'yer mean? He's never had
anything the matter with 'em!!'

53

'Hello old man, going in for gardening?'
'No, I'm making my own
cigarettes now!'

54

'What becomes of a car Mummy,
when it really won't go anymore?'
'Somebody sells it to your father!'

55

'Who's that woman that
smiled at you?'
'Now don't you start –
I've got enough trouble coming
explaining to her who *you* are!!'

INTEMPERANCE

"Drunkenness—Both drunkenness and teetotalism are *ipso facto* funny. Conventions:
i) All drunken men have optical illusions.
ii) Drunkenness is something peculiar to middle-aged men. Drunken youths or women are never represented."

George Orwell, 'The Art of Donald McGill'

56

'They had a beer drinking competition at the club last night.'
'Oh, who got second prize?'

57

58

59

Bless you Vicar, I <u>always</u>
know when I've had enough.
I fall down!

'Well, well, a few drinks make you
look quite beautiful!'
'But I haven't had a few drinks!'
'No, but I have!!!'

I think of you when far from home,
watching the breeze blow o'er the foam!

60

'My missus says she'll leave me if
I don't give up beer'
'Oh, I expect you'll miss her!'

61

But you don' understand Sir! I musht go
home. Your time'sh your own
but I've got to get up in the morning!

62

I'm high and dry on the coast here!

We're having a clinking time!

HUSSIES & FLOOZIES

"I have said that at least half of McGill's post cards are sex jokes, and a proportion, perhaps ten per cent, are far more obscene than anything else that is now printed in England. Newsagents are occasionally prosecuted for selling them, and there would be many more prosecutions if the broadest jokes were not invariably protected by double meanings...In England the gap between what can be said and what can be printed is rather exceptionally wide. Remarks and gestures which hardly anyone objects to on the stage would raise a public outcry if any attempt were made to reproduce them on paper. The comic post cards are the only existing exception to this rule, the only medium in which really 'low' humour is considered to be printable."

George Orwell, 'The Art of Donald McGill'

'Well, did the doctor find out what was the matter with you?'
'Oh, yes – he put his finger on the spot at once!'

66

The Price of a Kiss

A baby gets it for nothing

65

A young man steals it

An old man buys it

Have you one about three months old
that you could lend me for half an hour?
I'm just going to see my solicitor!

67

I'll be waiting for you!

69

68

The lord! The damsel 'as flown –
the bed 'as not been slept in,
the little chamber is empty!

So that's the sort of girl you are!
I might have found it out too late
At last my eyes are opened –
or one of 'em is at any rate!

70

'It's so different from yours! Did his
father have nice curly hair like this?'

'I don't know Ma'am,
he had his hat on!'

71

'A bottle of that scent, Madam,
and you have the men just where
you want 'em!'

'Well, you ought to be ashamed to sell it!'

72

It's not so much what she knows
that worries me –
It's how she got to know it!

73

'Was the child born in wed-lock?'
'No – in a black-out!'

74

Some girls work the whole week through
And wash their smalls on Sunday
Thank goodness I'm not one of them -
Well, not before next Monday!!

75

All the best things in life are free!!

76

'This boy of yours looks as strong
as a bull!'

'Don't know - I've never been cuddled
by a bull!'

77

My girl is short and slow
Jim's girl wears silky things
My girl wears calico
Jim's girl has wit and fun
My girl is dull and good
But d'you think I'd change my girl for Jims?
You bet I would!!

78

Where oh where's that sylph-like figure?
The slender waist, oh where is that?
Those ankles trim each day get bigger,
Darling you are getting fat!

79

80

81

Although you're all poshed up as fine,
You know you've nothing in the bank,
So I won't be your Valentine
For you can't keep a wife on swank!

A girl may look a perfect picture at night,
But a perfect sketch in the morning!

'You look pale tonight Mabel'
'Well, say something to make
me blush!'

82

83

84

'I'm very worried. My gal has got a
job in London at £9 a week.'
'Well, that's nothing to worry about!'
'Yes, but she's sending me ten!!'

'Here, Reggie, just hold Poogles a minute
while I go in and save the country!'

'Why don't you come for a walk across
the fields. Don't you trust me?
Or don't you trust yourself?'
'Yes I trust you and I trust myself,
but when we get together,
I wouldn't trust either of us!'

STOCK FIGURES

"Stock Figures. Foreigners seldom or never appear. The chief locality joke is the Scotsman, who is almost inexhaustible. The lawyer is always a swindler, the clergyman always a nervous idiot who says the wrong thing...Another survival is the Suffragette, one of the big jokes of the pre-1914 period and too valuable to be relinquished. She has reappeared, unchanged in physical appearance, as the Feminist lecturer or Temperance fanatic. A feature of the last few years is the complete absence of anti-Jew post cards. The 'Jew joke', always somewhat more ill-natured than the 'Scotch joke', disappeared abruptly soon after the rise of Hitler."

George Orwell, 'The Art of Donald McGill'

85

Take off yer ear-phones, Maggie – they're aboot tae tak' up the collection!

STOCK FIGURES

86

'Have you a "Bradshaw"?'
'Yes, Sir, – first door on the left!'

87

'You know I don't allow followers, Jane.'
'Why, Mum, I shouldn't have thought you'd
'ave any at your age!'

88

'I want to see the demon Drink –
I want to see the foul friend Drink!'
'Bill, go an' tell the sergeant major
that there's a bloke here wants to
stand 'im a pint!!'

STOCK FIGURES

90

89

Very uncertain weather ain't it? You reely
don't know what clothes to pawn!

92

Crickey, I must see that he gets his
shaving water punctual!

I may 'ave 'ad a couple, but, blimey!
I knows 'addock from 'ake!!

91

I'm down to my last tenner. If you don't send
me some cash I shall have to come home

93

Old or young, rich or poor, no one's safe from
that tongue of yours. When it once begins to wag,
nothing'll stop it but a fag!

94

Gosh that was a bad accident in Aberdeen!
A taxi-cab over-turned an' eight o' the
passengers were infused!!

95

Ye'd like a large port, eh?
Well, ye can be lookin' at ma bonny wee
photos of Southampton, whiles I get
masel' a drop o' whiskey!

96

Na, na, Maggie, I tell ye we will
hae an egg oor tea!
Dang it, we must let oorsels go sometimes!!

97

'Are you looking for the waiting room
Ma'am?'
'No I'm looking for a room where I shan't
have to wait!!'

98

'What's the matter Doctor?'
'Well, either you're dead or else my
stethescope is bunged up!'

99

This place suits me to a T
So blue the sky, so calm the C
Oh, how happy I should B
If you'd send me some...£sd.

STOCK FIGURES

100

101

102

Wearing glasses? And don't I need 'em!
Why, I gave the right change twice
yesterday!!

'Straight, old man, I can hardly
keep the wolf from the door'
'Keep it from the door!
Blimey, at my place it's come in an'
had pups on the mat!!'

She says to me 'come an' 'ave a fight' –
an' naturally I went, as any lady would!'

STOCK FIGURES

103

104

105

Though you waitresses swank
And fancy your weight,
You're glad of the penny
Left under the plate!

Some girls smile in the evening
Some girls smile at dawn
But the girl worth while
Is the one who'll smile
When her two front teeth are gone!

Peering round corners, listening at doors,
Everyone's business making is yours,
Looking for scandal when
there's none about
Your name's a Nosey Parker
without any doubt!

"...One sees what function these post cards, in their humble way, are performing. What they are doing is to give expression to the Sancho Panza view of life, the attitude to life that Miss Rebecca West once summed up as 'extracting as much fun as possible from smacking behinds in basement kitchens'...If you look into your own mind, which are you, Don Quixote or Sancho Panza? Almost certainly you are both. There is one part of you that wishes to be a hero or a saint, but another part of you is a little fat man who sees very clearly the advantages of staying alive with a whole skin. He is your unofficial self, the voice of the belly protesting against the soul. His tastes lie towards safety, soft beds, no work, pots of beer and women with 'voluptuous' figures. He it is who punctures your fine attitudes and urges you to look after Number One, to be unfaithful to your wife, to bilk your debts, and so on and so forth. Whether you allow yourself to be influenced by him is a different question."

George Orwell, 'The Art of Donald McGill'

106

**I sleep with my window open, as everybody should
And I get the sea breezes, where they do me most good!**

107

Just take this gentleman's
particulars down and look at
his testimonials!

108

'Ah! I've caught you – I just saw you
leaving the fishmongers!'
'My Love, I caught so many that I had
to sell some!'

109

The little swanker!
That's what he meant when he said
he was in the air force!!

110

'I want a hot bath this evening'
'Certainly Madam, I'll see you have it'

111

No more babies for me!
I'm getting married next week!!

112

I slept with something hot last night!

113

This is the finest watering-place on the canal!

114

Yes, Sir, if a lad's got anything in him,
the sea will fetch it out!

115

I'm sorry to see so few 'young mothers' here after all my efforts!

116

117

118

I **must** have another room. I've got a
big fat husband and three little ones
all sleeping in one bed!

'Poor Bill went home last night and
found his missus in bed with peritonitis.'
'Wot! D'yer mean that dam old ice-cream man
round the corner?'

Our handy man.
Does anything for anybody.
A real public convenience.

120

119

In case you're not feeling quite up to
scratch. I'm sending you this little present!

122

If a man has anything in him,
a sea trip will bring it out!'

Don't you think Dear, we ought to send
an extra blanket to Mrs Winterbottom?

121

I'm tickled to death here!

123

I know where I can get some good
information for the big race

124

'Who was best man at the wedding?'
'I was, but I didn't get a chance
to prove it!'

125

It's very full here, but I've got a nice
little room with coal and gas included!

126

He ain't half posh since he won the
football pool. Has had sleeve an' a tail
sewn on to his dicky!!

127

128

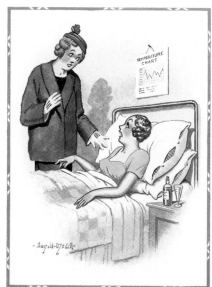

129

'Why is human milk better
than cow's milk?'
'Because it's cheaper, keeps better over the
week-end and the cat can't get at it!'

I went to the sales but all I got was
a compound fracture between the
'ladies underwear' and the
'bargain basement'!

'Isn't your eye watering Henry?'
'Yes, one of my pupils forgot to
put his hand up!'

130

'Get any orders today?'
'Yes, sir, two.'
'What were they?'
'Get out and stop out!!'

131

'He's got a glass eye'
'How do you know?'
'Oh it just came out in conversation!'

132

'What's the difference between the arial
an' the clothes line then?'
'Well, the arial draws the waves!'

133

I hope you didn't treat it roughly:
Remember you have a mother yourself!

134

Just wait till I cross the harbour bar!

135

'Dear me, what a very rude building!'
'Ah! You'd say so, Vicar, if you saw the writing on the walls inside!'

OUT OF THE MOUTHS OF BABES...

136

137

138

Naughty little cuss words
Hang dash and blow
Lead you on to wuss words,
Land you down below!

'Do you believe in Santa Claus?'
'Me? I've never met the man yet
that I believe in!'

If we have any children when
we're married,
I vote we have four at a time
and get their picture in the papers!

140

139

I may not be much of a dancer,
but I'm a good sitter out!

141

I feel ever so good - I must be bad!

My Daddy's very fond of animals too.
Yesterday he put his shirt on a
bleeding horse that was scratched!

142

What d'yer mean by coming on parade
with the top of your tunic undone!

143

I wish I was a rabbit!
They say they multiply rapidly!

144

'Not missed one Sunday school all the year.
I'm sure you deserve your prize!'

'Thank you Sir, but I think I'd have
preferred a book with a little
more sex in it!!'

145

'Mummy Is this really a Santa Claus?'
'No Dear, it's Daddy of course'
'And The Stork - is that Daddy too?'

146

'What do you know about
Queen Elizabeth?'
'She was called the Virgin Queen and
was a great success – as a queen!'

148

147

The Runny Nose

149

I likes 'em wild an' woolley!

"'Isiah' – what a funny name for
a teddy bear!'
'Well, you see one eye's 'igher
than the other!'

150

'So I don't look like an old woman now
I've had my hair cut short, eh Bobby?'
'No - you look like an old man!'

151

'What a nice little dog you have!'
'It isn't a dog, Sir, it's a rude word!!'

OUT OF THE MOUTHS OF BABES...

153

152

Mother told me I shouldn't get
picked up by strange men!

155

Mother says this book is not fit for a young
girl to read - I quite agree with her!

Our tom cat, don't you see
Brought his kittens home to tea
We were rather surprised at that
For we didn't think he was
That sort of cat

154

I call my doggie 'Corsets' - 'cos he's
tied up all day and let out at night!

156

'Cheer up, there are plenty
more fish in the sea.'
'Yes, but I don't want to marry a fish!'

158

157

'No, Mrs Smith, you said a baby an'
I've brought a baby. It's too late to
change it for a kitten now!'

159

The Little Boxers

Whose fault is it you haven't got a boy?
Whose fault is it you're walking all alone?
Whose fault is it? Why, say, i'm telling you,
It's no one's fault at all - but just your own!

160

What's cooking?

161

The trouble is with me is
I fall in love too easily!

162

You'll be glad to know we arrived safely

GREETINGS CARDS

164

163

A Merry Christmas to you
May every Christmas joy be yours
With jolly games for out of doors
Bright fires and Christmas fare at home
And lots more Christmases to come

It's long since Noah was in the ark
It's long since Caesar landed here
Since Shakespeare wrote it's quite a while
Queen Anne's been dead for many a year.
It's years and years it strikes me too,
Since I have had a line from you.

165

Birthday Greetings
I send this card with all my love,
And that is all I have to say
Except of course the old, old wish
'Many happy returns of the day!'

166

Good luck on your Birthday

167

May you have just one bit of good luck
after another!

GREETINGS CARDS

169

168

Though far apart I'm always thinking of you

171

I've just slipped down to the post with my Christmas greeting to you!

With love for your birthday
I'm just popping out to put this in the post
To wish you all joy and of presents a host
May your birthday be happy as e'er can be found
And a jolly good year till
The next one comes round

170

'Do your good deed for the day –
and drop me a line

172

I'm always singing your praises
when you're away!

SOLDIERS & WARTIME

"I never read the proclamations of generals before battle, the speeches of führers and prime ministers, the solidarity songs of public schools and left-wing political parties...without seeming to hear in the background a chorus of raspberries from all the millions of common men to whom these high sentiments make no appeal. Any contemporary event, cult or activity which has comic possibilities...rapidly finds its way into the picture post cards, but their general atmosphere is extremely old-fashioned. The implied political outlook is a Radicalism appropriate to about the year 1900. The European situation only began to reflect itself in them at some time in 1939... A few express anti-Hitler sentiments of a not very vindictive kind. Unlike the twopenny weekly papers, comic post cards are not the product of any great monopoly company, and evidently they are not regarded as having any importance in forming public opinion. There is no sign in them of any attempt to induce an outlook acceptable to the ruling class."

George Orwell, 'The Art of Donald McGill'

173

A blow on the Siegfried line!

174

That's where Dad is!

175

Good luck to my boy in air force blue!

176

I should think so indeed!
The hussy ought to be interned!!

177

178

179

When this card shall reach you Dear,
Though I'm far out at sea,
You'll know that I still think of you
And hope you think of me

Don't ever feel alone, my dear,
Though we are far apart
Wherever you may chance to be
I'm there in thought and heart!

Don't forget me, Dearest,
That's all I ask of you
Send me a line with greetings kind
Just as I send to you

180

And my address is c/o the G.P.O.!!

181

Good night, Dad!

182

'An' I hope it chokes 'im!'

184

183

My number's up!

186

**I'm somewhere in France, but of course
I mustn't tell you exactly where!**

**Our sergeant major's a nice man –
but he ain't half a chatterbox!**

185

Keep smiling!

187

I'm just sew-sew at present!

188

And give my kind regards to
all the poor civilians!

189

Little girls like to play with painted dolls
And little boys like to play with soldiers.
When they grow up,
The girls like to play with soldiers
And the boys like to play with painted dolls!

190

Yes Major, my men would follow me
anywhere!

Don't cry darlings! There are plenty of girls at...

"The comic post cards are one expression of his point of view, a humble one, less important than the music halls, but still worthy of attention. In a society which is still basically Christian they naturally concentrate on sex jokes; in a totalitarian society, if they had any freedom of expression at all, they would probably concentrate on laziness or cowardice, but at any rate on the unheroic in one form or another. It will not do to condemn them on the ground that they are vulgar and ugly. That is exactly what they are meant to be. Their whole meaning and virtue is in their unredeemed low-ness, not only in the sense of obscenity, but lowness of outlook in every direction whatever. The slightest hint of 'higher' influences would ruin them utterly. They stand for the worm's-eye view of life, for the music-hall world where marriage is a dirty joke or a comic disaster, where the rent is always behind and the clothes are always up the spout, where the lawyer is always a crook and the Scotsman always a miser, where the newly-weds make fools of themselves on the hideous beds of seaside lodging-houses and the drunken, red-nosed husbands roll home at four in the morning to meet the linen-nightgowned wives who wait for them behind the front door, poker in hand. Their existence, the fact that people want them, is symptomatically important. Like the music halls, they are a sort of saturnalia, a harmless rebellion against virtue. They express only one tendency in the human mind, but a tendency which is always there and will find its own outlet, like water. On the whole, human beings want to be good, but not too good, and not quite all the time."

George Orwell, 'The Art of Donald McGill'